The Art of Sugarcraft

PIPING

NORMA LAVER

Foreword Mitzie Wilson
Series Editor Joyce Becker
Photography by Melvin Grey and Graham Tann

CHANCELLOR
PRESS

VωM

Published in 1996 by Chancellor Press
an imprint of Reed Books Ltd
Michelin House, 81 Fulham Road
London SW3 6RB
and Auckland, Melbourne, Singapore and Toronto

By arrangement with Merehurst Limited
Ferry House, 51-57 Lacy Road, London, SW15 1PR
© Copyright 1986 Merehurst Limited

ISBN 1-85152-961-6

Designed by Carole Perks
Editorial Assistant Suzanne Ellis
Further assistance provided by Trudie Ballantyne,
Rachel Lalley and Sara Townsend
Cover photograph by Graham Tann
Typeset by Filmset & Clive Dorman & Co.
Colour separation by Fotographics Ltd, U.K. – Hong Kong
Printed in Italy

14.95

CONTENTS

NORMA LAVER

FOREWORD

As a keen cake decorator myself, I have found Norma Laver's piping instructions invaluable. The piping on a cake can make or mar your design, and although I have a reasonably steady hand I do find it difficult to get perfect results every time. Now her instructions have taught me where I'm going wrong. There's no need for an amateur attempt at writing Happy Birthday, as the book gives patterns for all your favourite greetings, templates for script and lettering styles, with illustrations to help everyone master the skills.

From basic shell piping, Norma's techniques show how to build up the most intricate of borders, elegant run-out collars, dainty drop lines, curves and the finest extension work. Now I know how to do them all, and although I can't promise you'll reach the same standard as Norma, it only takes practice for you too to become perfect.

My favourite sections of the book must be how to embroider in icing, with patterns to copy, beautiful broderie anglaise, tulle and lace work, too. This book is a delight for beginners and professional cake icers alike.

Mitzie Wilson
Editor, B.B.C. Good Food Magazine

It is difficult to believe that Norma Laver only began cake decorating in 1979. An accomplished craftswoman, she enrolled in a beginner's class and she took to this new medium with enthusiasm and delight. Her great talent for sugarart was confirmed when she won the very first competition she entered, just 18 months after her first icing lesson. She has since collected many more awards at national and international levels.

Cake decorating dominates the Laver household. Norma's daughters, Alison and Karen, are both enthusiasts, and even her husband has been known to pick up a piping tube and help finish a cake. Norma is co-owner of a shop specializing in cake decorating equipment and she works as a teaching assistant in a local primary school. She teaches sugarcraft in adult education and she is in great demand to design cakes for brides all over the UK.

Norma takes great pleasure in decorating a cake, but she is happy that the cake will be cut and eaten, gaining satisfaction from this artistic yet functional craft. Norma is an expert in many of the decorating skills and particularly enjoys fine piping. She is well known in the sugarcraft world for her extension work and embroidery.

EQUIPMENT

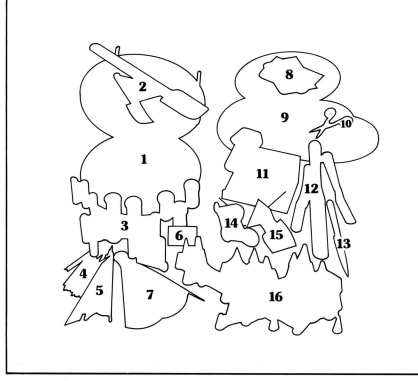

EQUIPMENT

Piping tubes come in a variety of qualities and prices but to achieve good results, especially with fine work, the best quality tubes are worth the extra expense. Flower tubes (No56 and 59) are necessary for piped flowers. Basket weave or ribbon tubes are also handy.

No0 and No00 are used for extension work, lace, and other fine work. No1 is used for embroidery and writing. No5 is the first of the stars. These are all useful for borders and edges, or when it is necessary to decorate a cake quickly. The larger stars can be used with buttercream. No23 is a basket tube.

Small palette knives and side scrapers are useful for mixing colour into icing.

For sifting icing sugar use a fine meshed sieve kept for this purpose only.

An electric mixer is useful for beating royal icing.

You will also need greaseproof paper, wax paper and baking parchment.

Colour is brushed onto decorated cakes with various sizes of paint brushes.

A sharp knife is needed for cutting icing bags; scissors are also useful.

A scriber or glass-headed pins are used to mark a design onto an iced cake.

A good turntable, tilting if possible, is important.

An anglepoise lamp provides good light and can be moved easily. It is also useful for drying lace and flood work.

This is a selection of tools and equipment used for piping. Most are ordinary kitchen or household items, while the more unusual tools are available from cake decorating shops and specialist suppliers.

1 Turntable
2 Rubber spatulas for buttercream
3 Paste colours and petal dust
4 Cocktail sticks
5 Paintbrushes
6 Glass-headed pins
7 Scribers
8 Side scrapers
9 Cake boards
10 Scissors
11 Icing bag stand
12 Palette knives
13 Sharp paring knife
14 Icing nails
15 Forms for piping shapes
16 Piping tubes

PIPING BAGS

Well-made piping bags from greaseproof paper or baking parchment are essential for good piping. Paper bags are easier to control than the plastic or metal icing syringes, and they are disposable, so do not have to be cleaned like the plastic or nylon bags.

Piping bags should never be made too large, as they will be difficult to control and the heat from your hand will change the consistency of the icing. Bags for buttercream will need to be larger than those for royal icing. If doing a lot of piping, make several bags before starting to pipe. If piping with different coloured icing or when using different tubes, you will need several bags on hand for each one.

There are different methods for making paper piping bags. The one shown here produces bags which are a good shape and easy to use.

Cut along the fold with a sharp knife to make two right-angle triangles.

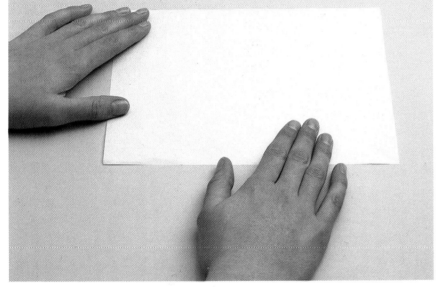

Cut a piece of greaseproof paper twice as long as it is wide.

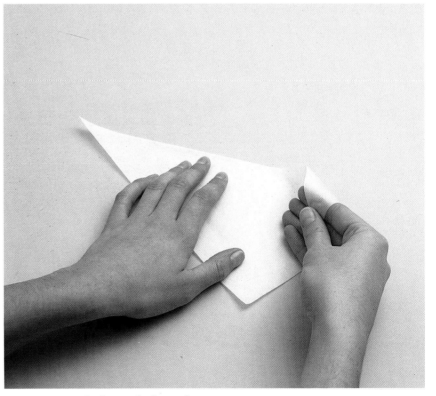

Lay the triangle flat with the right angle facing you and fold the corner inwards.

Fold the paper diagonally. The points will not meet.

Place the corner on the point of
the right angle, making a cone.

Wrap the corner around the cone
twice so that the points meet.

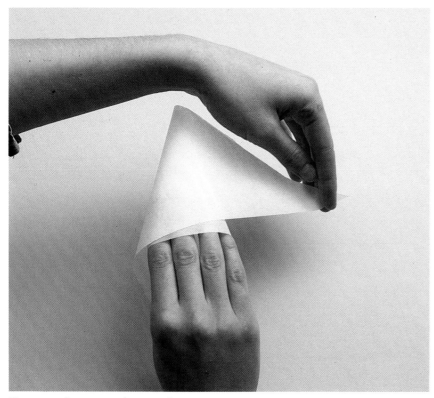

Put your fingers in the cone to
hold it and bring the other corner
over it.

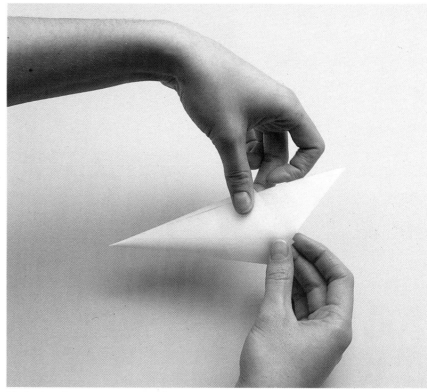

Slide the three points together to
tighten the bag.

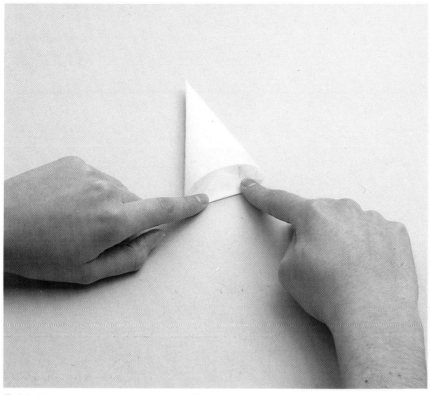

Fold the top point into the bag. If piping without a tube, fill the bag now.

If using a piping tube, cut off the tip of the bag with scissors and insert the tube.

FILLING THE BAG

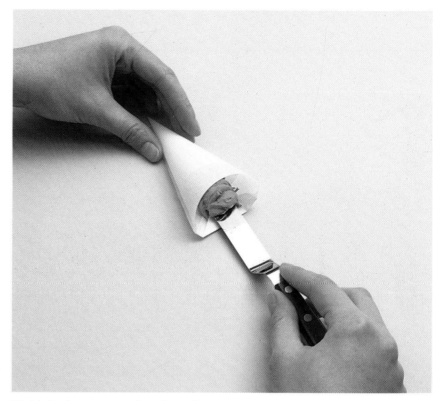

Hold the bag in your hand or place on the table and hold the point. Scoop up some icing with a palette knife and place in the bag.

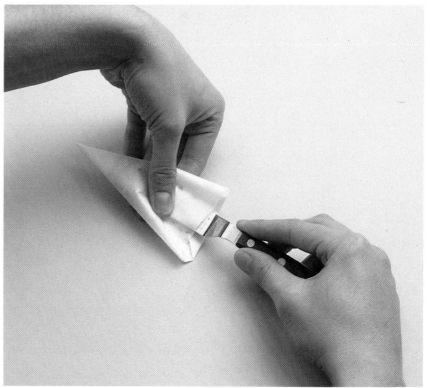

Hold the top of the bag down and gently pull out the palette knife.

Fold the points of the bag towards the centre.

Fasten by folding the top of the bag over twice.

USING A PIPING BAG

The bag when filled will fit comfortably into one hand. The other is then left free to steady it.

Hold the bag as you would hold a short, very fat pencil, with the thumb and index finger either side and the third finger bent underneath. The fourth and fifth fingers are also bent under. The folded end of the bag will then fit snugly into the hand between the thumb and index finger.

For smaller amounts of icing the bag will not reach as far as the palm, so hold it with the thumb and first two fingers. Always make sure the thumb is on the folded end, keeping the bag firmly closed.

If this position seems uncomfortable at first, persevere, as it enables the most pressure to be applied with the least effort. This is very important if you are piping for a long time.

Pressure is applied by the thumb and first two fingers which are in contact with the bag. Fine movement is also achieved by use of these fingers.

Do not hold the bag with both hands as this restricts movement and control. If two hands are necessary to force the icing through the nozzle, then it is too stiff or has been made incorrectly.

ICING FOR PIPING

Royal Icing

200g (7oz/1¾cups) icing (confectioner's) sugar, sifted
white of 1 large egg
pinch of tartaric acid (cream of tartar)

Put all the ingredients in a grease-free bowl of an electric mixer. Stir to incorporate, then mix for about 5 minutes on medium.

It is important that all the equipment be clean and free of grease or fat, so unless the mixer is used only for making royal icing, scald all of the equipment and dry before use.

If, when separating the egg white from the yolk, the yolk breaks, discard the white and use another egg. Any trace of fat from the yolk will make the icing flat.

Colouring royal icing: Royal icing can be coloured with liquid or paste food colours, but paste colours are preferable because they give a dense colour without altering the consistency of the icing.
    When colouring a small amount of icing for piping, put the icing on a side scraper. Add colour and use a palette knife to blend in the colour with a backwards and forwards motion. If colouring a large amount of icing, colour some on a scraper first, then incorporate this into the bowl of icing.
    Liquid colours are useful if a colour is to be repeated. Use an eyedropper to add the colour until the desired shade is reached, then record how many drops were added to the amount of icing.

Buttercream Icing

240g (8oz/2cups) icing (confectioner's) sugar
60-120g (2-4oz/¼-½cup) butter, margarine, or white fat
milk or water as required

Cream butter or margarine very well. Add half of the sieved icing sugar gradually, beating well after each addition. Add the rest of the sugar spoonful by spoonful, adding liquid if required alternately, until the mixture is smooth and fluffy and will hold its shape.

Buttercream for piping is best made with about 60g (2oz/¼cup) icing sugar. Add liquid to achieve the right consistency.

When piping with buttercream, the heat of your hand changes the consistency of the icing very quickly, especially when doing basketwork. Minimise this by using a small amount in a small bag, and keep replacing the bags.

BASKET WEAVE CAKE

For a round cake top or for the lid
of a round basket, pipe lines like
the spokes of a wheel. The basket
work lines will be very short at the
centre and longer at the outside.
Pipe them so that they appear to
go over and under the spokes.

BASIC PIPING

Writing tubes

To pipe a straight line work towards your body. Touch the tube to the cake surface and apply light, even pressure, pulling away immediately to avoid making a bulb at the beginning of the line. Lift the tube up and about 3cm (1½in) away from the surface. Keep your eye on the line to be followed. When about 3cm (1½in) from the end of the line, stop the pressure and gently lower the tube into position. With practice you will be able to finish the piped line in exactly the right place.

When piping a line with angles, such as a zigzag, touch the nozzle to the surface of the cake each time you change direction.

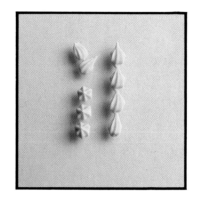

No6 star tube.

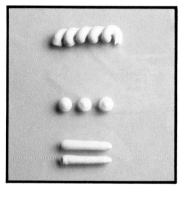

No4 writing tube.

No15 star tube.

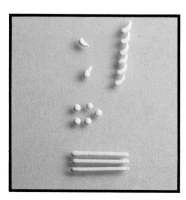

No3 writing tube.

No9 star tube.

No2 writing tube.

No12 star tube.

No42 shell tube.

Petal and basket-weave tubes

No44 shell tube.

No56 flower or petal tube.

No5 shell tube.

No7 star tube.

No59 flower or petal tube.

No23 basket weave tube.

No8 star tube.

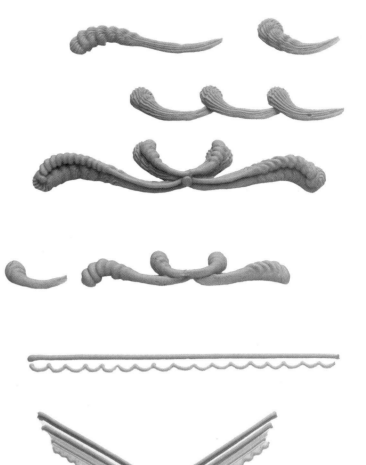

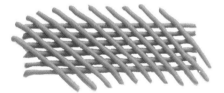

Top to bottom: Shells; running scrolls; pulled shells; shells; S scroll; dropline work; straight line work; trellis work.

Top to bottom: S scroll and C scroll; running C scroll; S and C scroll with overpiping; C scroll and S and C scroll; straight and scallop lines; straight line work.

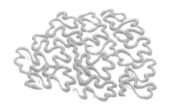

Top to bottom: S and C scroll combination with reverse S and C; herringbone; running S scroll with overpiping.

Top to bottom: Shells; running S scroll; herringbone; curved lines; petit point lace work; cornelli work.

CORNELLI WORK CAKE

Cornelli work looks attractive done in a contrasting colour and is useful for hiding a poor cake surface. Cornelli work is simply a continuous wavy line piped with a No0 or No1 writing tube. Work on a small area at a time keeping the line equidistant from any others. Bend the line up and down and from side to side, varying it all the time. If you find this difficult, practise by drawing a line on paper first, and then piping over it.

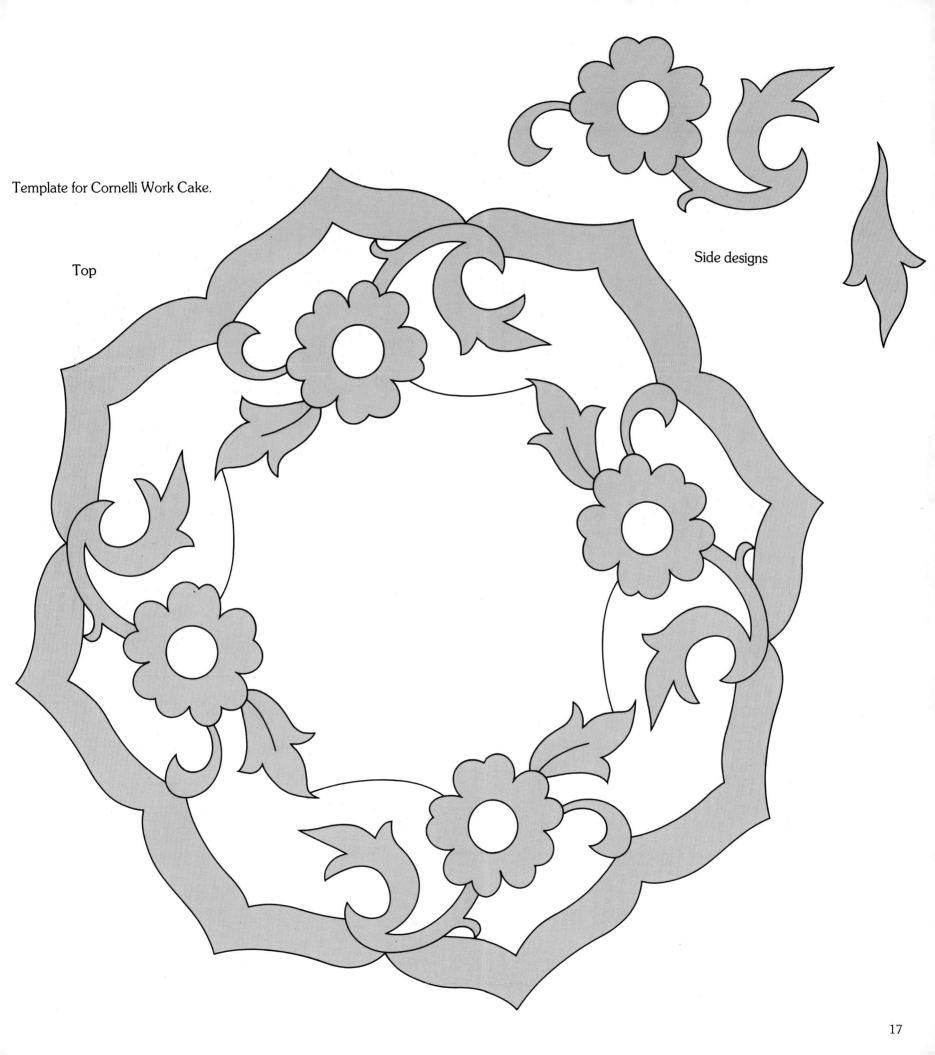

Template for Cornelli Work Cake.

Top

Side designs

BIRDS

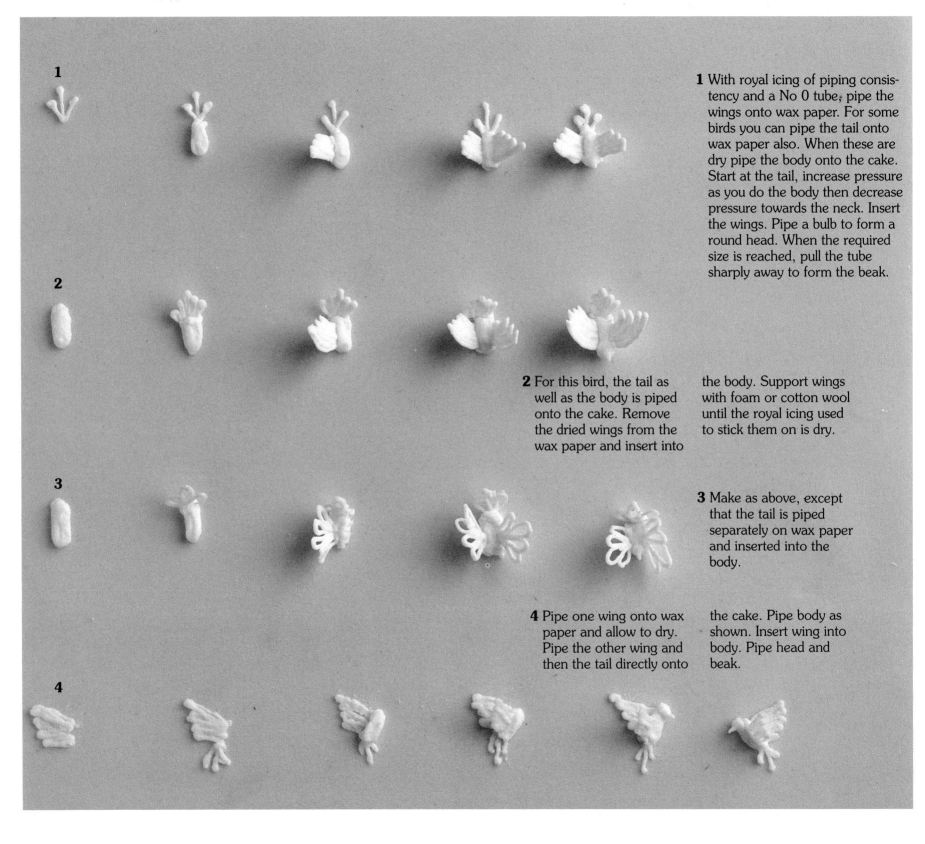

1 With royal icing of piping consistency and a No 0 tube, pipe the wings onto wax paper. For some birds you can pipe the tail onto wax paper also. When these are dry pipe the body onto the cake. Start at the tail, increase pressure as you do the body then decrease pressure towards the neck. Insert the wings. Pipe a bulb to form a round head. When the required size is reached, pull the tube sharply away to form the beak.

2 For this bird, the tail as well as the body is piped onto the cake. Remove the dried wings from the wax paper and insert into the body. Support wings with foam or cotton wool until the royal icing used to stick them on is dry.

3 Make as above, except that the tail is piped separately on wax paper and inserted into the body.

4 Pipe one wing onto wax paper and allow to dry. Pipe the other wing and then the tail directly onto the cake. Pipe body as shown. Insert wing into body. Pipe head and beak.

PIPING SHAPES OVER A MOULD

Many objects are suitable for this work, and there are many commercial moulds available. If fine work is to be done, the article must be fairly small. The design must be piped freehand.

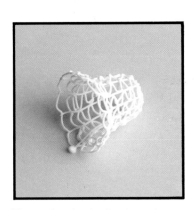

To make the bells, first draw around the base of the bell. Divide this circle into equal sections. Grease the outside of the mould with white fat (shortening). Place the mould on the pattern as a guide for the vertical lines. Pipe the lines from top to bottom, dividing the bell into equal sections. Fill in the spaces with an S-design or freehand flowers or, if the lines are closer together, dots. Make sure the lines touch each other. Leave to dry. When dry, warm the shape slightly to melt the fat and release the filigree shape.

AUTUMN LEAVES
BIRTHDAY CAKE

Happy Birthday

RUN-OUT COLLARS WITH BRUSH EMBROIDERY

Trace the designs for the borders and collars, place on a board, cover with wax paper, and pipe the outlines using gold-coloured royal icing and a No1 tube. Flood with soft royal icing and leave to dry. Make four of each design. Colour the leaves with brush embroidery. Flooding the colours with the gold icing first makes them strong so that the deep autumn colours can be added afterwards. Position the borders and collars on the cake and attach with gold royal icing.

SLEEPING MOUSE CAKE

GREEN RUN-OUT COLLARS

Trace the designs and make four
top collars and four base collars.
Leave to dry for about two days
before attaching to the cake.

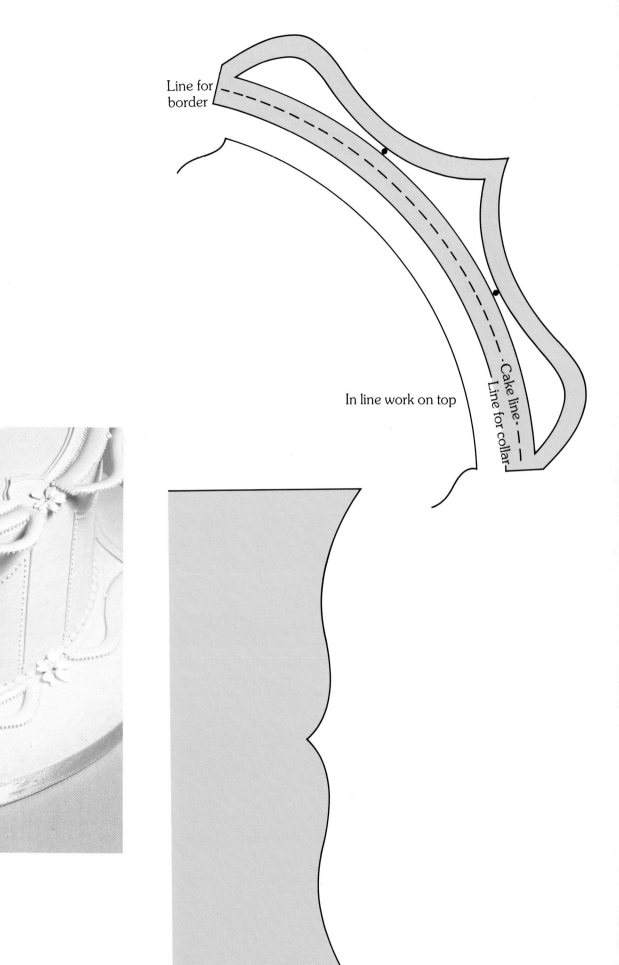

Line for
border

In line work on top

Cake line
Line for collar

Side design

RUN-OUT GREENHOUSE

Trace the pattern pieces and place under wax paper. Outline all the pieces with a No1 tube and green royal icing, then flood with soft royal icing. Let dry. Lie the front down and attach door. Pipe a line of royal icing for hinge. Position the door and support with foam rubber until dry.

Attach front to sides and sides to back, making sure the base lines match the plan with angles of 90°. When dry, attach the roof, side pieces and, finally, the top piece.

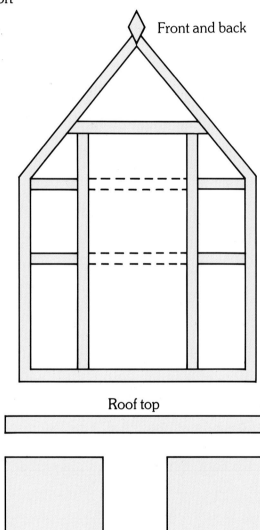

Front and back

Roof top

Base

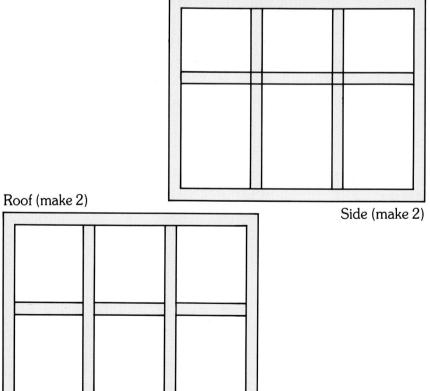

Roof (make 2)

Side (make 2)

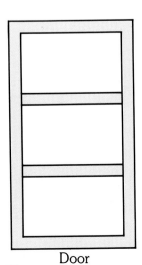

Door

STAR, SHELL AND TASSEL BORDERS

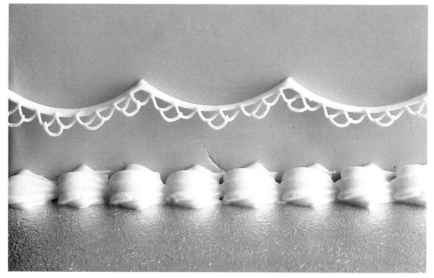

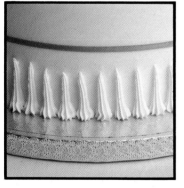

Use a star tube for tassel borders. Lean over the cake and pipe a rosette on the board. Bring the tube up towards you to a height of 3cm (1¼in), decreasing the pressure to make the tassel shape.

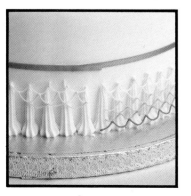

If wished, pipe drop loops in different colours from one tassel to the next. Use a fine tube. The design shown here features the four colours in the brush embroidery on the Anemone Cake.

Any shell tube can be used for this technique. Hold the tube at a 45° angle to the cake. Squeeze to form a shell, pull to the right (to the left if you are left-handed) while releasing pressure. Hold the nozzle at this position to pipe the next shell.

The shell border is overpiped with a circle using a No00 tube. Circle scratch line on board.

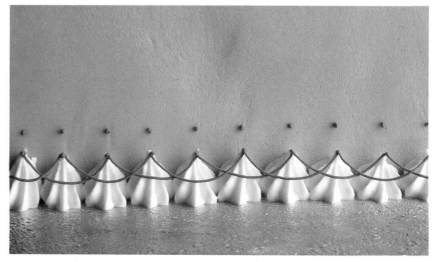

Pipe the shells vertically with the points at the top. Drop loops from the top of alternate points.

TOP DESIGNS

Designs for the tops of cakes can be piped directly onto the cake, or onto sugarpaste or royal icing plaques. Although a very experienced decorator will be able to pipe some designs freehand, most require a template. An advantage of piping the design onto a prepared plaque is that the plaque can be removed before the cake is cut and saved as a momento or stored for reuse.

Trace the design onto greaseproof or tracing paper, then transfer to the plaque or cake by lightly marking with pins or a scriber.

A simple trellis design piped freehand on a sugarpaste plaque. Pipe the trellis first. When dry, position piped royal icing roses and pipe on the stems and leaves.

The top design for the Sleeping Mouse Cake, which is piped directly onto the surface of the royal-iced cake. Transfer the design to the cake, then begin by piping the leaves which will appear furthest away when the design is finished. Build up the design with pressure piping. Add in detail with a fine tube when the icing is dry.

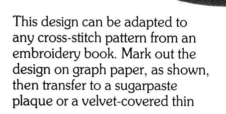

An unusual geometric design piped on a plaque. Use the design here for a pattern, or create a different design with a compass or by tracing different shapes. First, pipe the outlines with a fine tube. Pipe the diagonal lines, first in one direction and then in the other direction. Fill in the sections with cornelli work. Pipe tiny dots around the edge of the star.

This design can be adapted to any cross-stitch pattern from an embroidery book. Mark out the design on graph paper, as shown, then transfer to a sugarpaste plaque or a velvet-covered thin cake card. Pipe the background first, so that the finished design resembles needlepoint embroidery. Pipe the chosen design in cross-stitch.

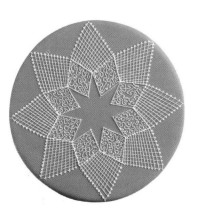

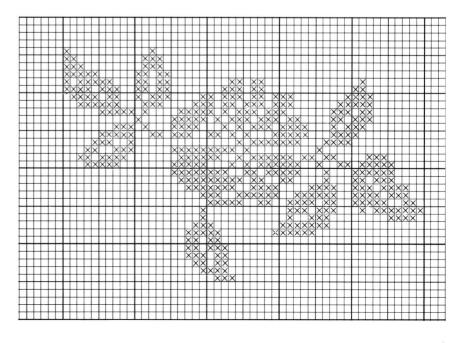

PIPED ROSES

Use stiff royal icing. Attach wax paper to nail and hold in left hand. Hold the petal tube vertically with the broad end of the tube towards the centre of the nail. Keep the broad end on the paper and lift the narrow end of the tube until the bag is at a 90° angle.

Finish by turning the tube flat and pulling away. For the third petal, repeat as for the second petal beginning slightly higher up the cone, and starting at the opposite side.

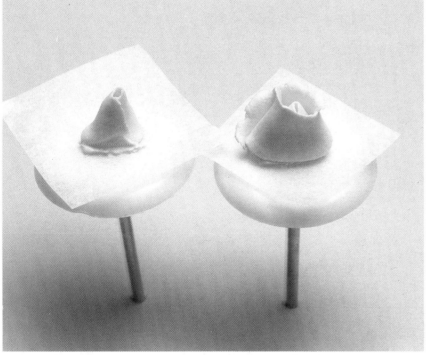

Lift the tube from the paper and turn the nail clockwise to make a cone. When you have made a complete rotation, turn the tube so that it lies flat and pull away.

For the second petal, hold the bag at a 90° angle with the broad end of the tube at the bottom. Begin part way up at the back of the cone, turn the nail clockwise and pipe a band around the cone, lifting and lowering as you go.

The tube is held horizontal and upsidedown for the fourth petal.

Lift the tube up and turn it over while moving the nail clockwise.

The fifth and sixth petals are made in the same way, each slightly overlapping the one before.

The finished rose.

MORE PIPED FLOWERS ON NAILS

Use stiff royal icing for all flowers. Attach a small square of wax paper to the nail with royal icing. Keep the square small or it will get in your way. Left-handers should reverse these instructions.

Pansy: Pipe the first and second petals as for forget-me-nots. The third petal is in front and just to the left of the first petal. The fourth petal is in front and to the right of the second petal. To make petal five, start halfway over petal four. Pipe a semicircle to finish, halfway over petal three. Paint the markings with food colour.

Apple blossom: Pipe as for forget-me-not but finish with piped green dots.

Narcissus: Pipe white petals with the tube flat as for forget-me-not, but move tube out and in again to get the correct length. Pipe the first three petals an even distance apart. Pipe the next three petals in the gaps. Pinch each petal at the end or stroke it with a paintbrush. Pipe the centre with a No1 tube. First pipe the pistil by pulling out a dot in the centre. Then pipe a spiral around it to form the trumpet. Finish with a zigzag line at the top. Paint with orange food colour.

Forget-me-not: Place royal icing in the bag, white on the broad side of the tube and blue on the narrow side.
Hold the bag horizontally with the broad side of the tube at the centre of the nail. Squeeze the bag and move your right hand in a clockwise direction while your left hand turns the nail in an anticlockwise direction. Move through almost one-quarter of a circle. Stop the pressure and finish with a slicing movement towards the centre of the flower. The second and subsequent petals overlap the preceding one and the fifth petal is piped over the first. Finish with a small piped yellow dot.

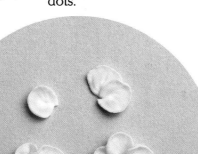

Primrose: Use pale yellow royal icing. Follow the instructions for piping the forget-me-not, but halfway around each petal move the nozzle in towards the centre and then out again. When the flowers are dry, paint or petal dust the centres a darker yellow. Pipe a white dot in each centre.

FLOWER BASKET

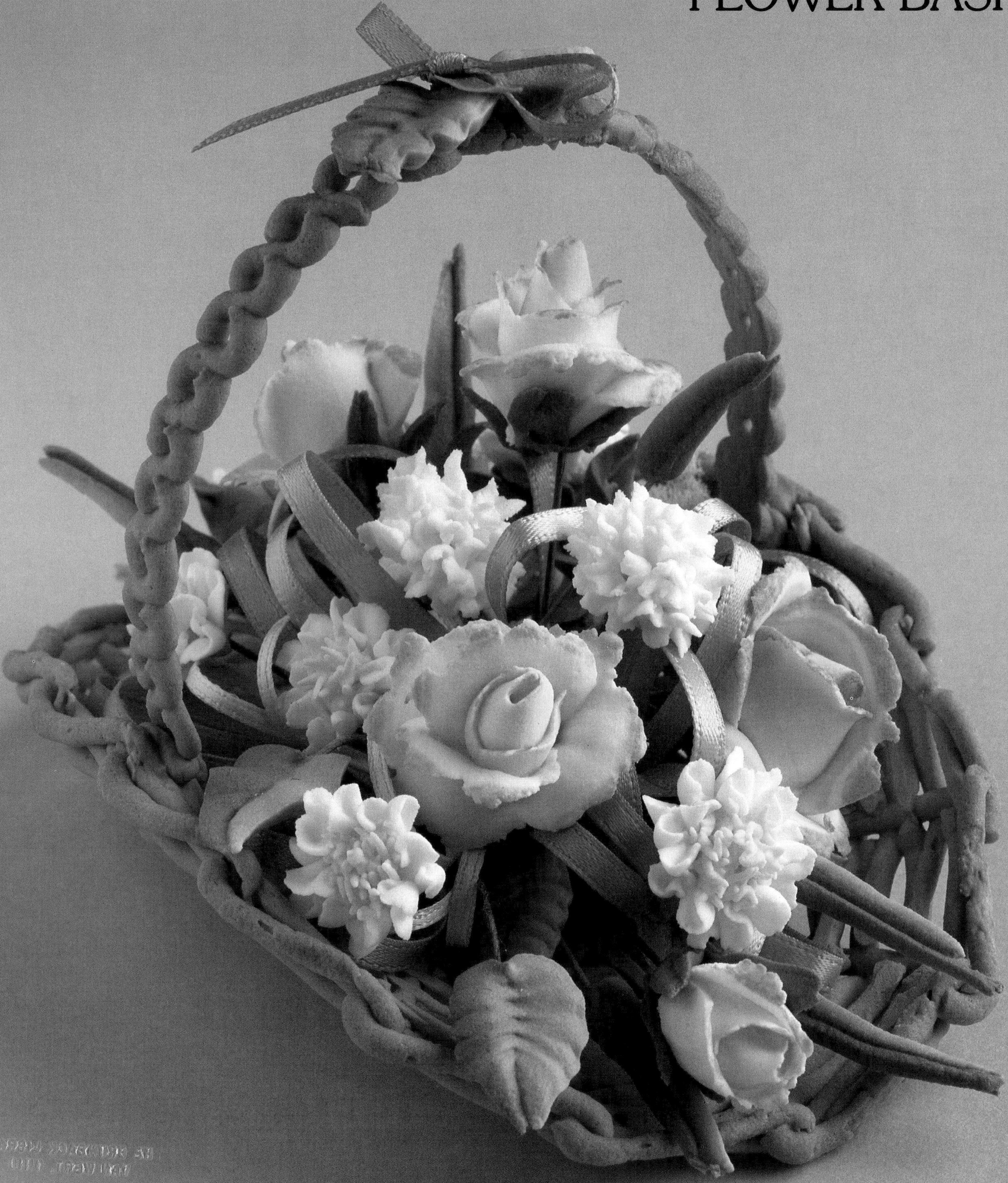

WIRED PIPED FLOWERS AND BASKET

Use 24-gauge flower wire. Make a hook at one end. Fill a bag fitted with a No4 tube with firm peak royal icing. Insert the hook into the tube and squeeze while withdrawing the wire to coat the hook with icing. Push the hook into the tube a distance equal to the height of the flower you plan to make. Allow to dry. For the rest of the piping use a flower tube. Never insert the wires directly into a cake or use wired flowers on children's cakes.

Leaves: Lay a piece of straight wire on wax paper. Fill bag with two shades of green icing and cut the end into a sharp V-shaped point. The more of the bag you slice off, the larger the leaves will be. Pipe a leaf, making sure the tip of the leaf covers one end of the wire. For smooth long leaves, move the tube quickly. For wavy leaves either move the bag slightly from side to side or up and down. Experiment to get different effects.

Carnation: Hold the wire vertically and the icing bag horizontally with the narrow end of the tube uppermost along the centre. Turn the wire clockwise while applying pressure to the bag and moving the tube up and down. Continue until the flower is the size you require. Dry for a few minutes. Snip the petals with small scissors. Pipe the calyx with a bag cut for making leaves.

Daisy: Pipe a short blob onto the wire with a No4 tube. Allow to dry. With a No1 tube pipe a series of pulled dots in yellow to cover the blob.
Fill a small flower tube with white icing. Hold the flower upside-down and pipe the outside petals with an out and in motion.

Piped basket: Tape oval pattern to the side of a bottle and tape wax paper over the pattern. Pipe basket work with a No2 tube. Neaten the top edge with piped interlinked S-designs. Pipe a handle over the bottle, also with an interlinked S-design. The handle should extend as far around the bottle as the basket extends. When dry, remove the pieces from the bottle and fill basket with flowers arranged in sugarpaste. Stick the handle in place with royal icing.

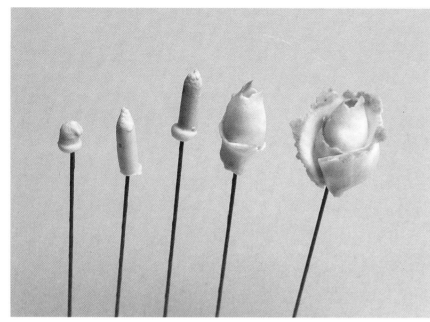

COCKTAIL STICK FLOWERS

These flowers will add height to a cake. Stick them straight into the cake. If the cocktail stick forms the stem of the flower, colour it green with food colour before piping. Pipe leaves along the stick starting at the bottom. Add the flowers, which can be copies of real flowers or imaginary ones. For the white or yellow bell flowers, use a No1 tube and make a circular movement to create the bell shape.

Yellow rose: Pipe a long blob on the hook with a No4 tube. With the narrow edge of a flower tube held uppermost hold the icing bag horizontally next to the icing blob. Twist the wire clockwise while applying an even pressure to the bag. Pipe all the way around, then gradually lower the tube to form a bud. Stop the pressure when your fingers have twisted the wire as far as they can.

Pipe the second petal with the narrow end of the tube leaning slightly away from vertical. Pipe around while twisting the bud clockwise. Lift the tube up and then down to complete the turn. Pipe the third petal in the same way, starting opposite the end of the second petal.

For petals four and five, hold the bag horizontally, with the broad end of the tube touching the base of the flower and the narrow end at the left. Your hand should have the palm facing down.

Squeeze while turning your hand holding the bag through 180° and twist the flower clockwise with the other hand. Each petal should overlap the preceding one slightly. Pipe the calyx with a bag cut in a V-shape as for piping leaves.

Sunflowers: Pipe the flowers onto wax paper on a nail, using a small flower tube and stiff yellow icing. Hold the tube at right angles to and almost touching the nail. Squeeze and pull the petal sharply towards the centre. Work a circle of petals leaving a space in the centre. Fill the space with brown dots. When dry stick the flower to a cocktail stick which already has leaves attached.

LACE

The addition of lace to a cake immediately gives it a delicate look. Lace is the last decoration to go on a cake, as it is very fragile. Always use fresh, well beaten royal icing or the lace will not be strong and will break as soon as it is picked up.

When choosing your design, remember that lace which looks simple may not always be the easiest to do. If it has just a few straight lines any flaws will show, whereas a more complicated design could mask faults.

Place the lace pattern onto a flat surface and masking tape a piece of wax paper over it. A very thin smear of white fat on the wax paper helps to release the dried lace. If the lace has a straight line where it joins the cake, pipe this first, then the rest of the pattern. Always pipe more pieces than you will need to allow for breakages. When dry, the lace should come away easily. A slight movement of the paper should be enough to release the pieces, or use a thin palette knife or a fine brush. Pick up lace with your fingers (it is impossible to do this with tweezers) and attach to the cake with two dots of royal icing per section. This icing should also be fresh, well beaten to full peak or the pieces will not stay in place.

Lace patterns

TWENTY-FIRST BIRTHDAY CAKE

BASIC EMBROIDERY

Piped embroidery is a series of straight and curved lines, dots, leaf and flower shapes etc, put together in a design.

When doing embroidery on the side of a cake it is much easier if you tilt it away from yourself.

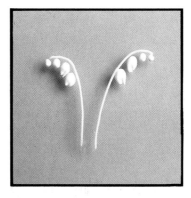

Lily of the valley: For all methods, pipe a stem first. Pipe oval bulbs of icing. Clean the end of the tube, insert into the centre of the bulb and pull downwards sharply. Buds are graduated oval bulbs.

Pipe an oval bulb with three piped dots beneath.

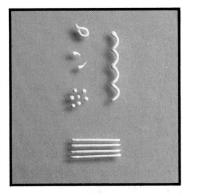

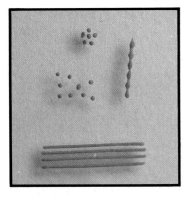

Dots: Piped dots should not have points so keep the icing soft. Just touch the tube to the cake surface, apply pressure and stop when the dot is the required size.

Pulled dots: Pipe dot then pull the tube away to the side.

Leaf shape: Start at the point, curve around and finish neatly. The sides can be curved slightly or more deeply as in a teardrop.

Flowers: These can be five dots piped around one dot; pulled dots around one dot; or leaf shapes piped in a circle, pointing in or out.

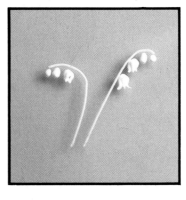

Think of an elephant! Pipe one 'ear' — a pulled curved dot. Pipe the second 'ear' — a reversed curved pulled dot. Then pipe the 'trunk' — squeezed in between the 'ears'. Press towards the cake and then sharply out again.

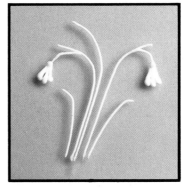

Snowdrops: Pipe three teardrops with a bulb at the top.

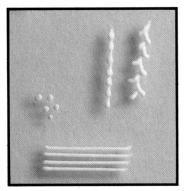

TUBE EMBROIDERY

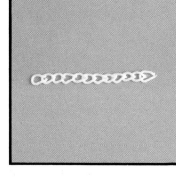

Chainstitch: Pipe an open teardrop. Pipe a second open teardrop starting inside the open end of the first.

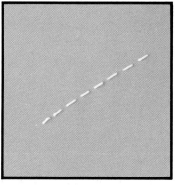

Running stitch: Pipe short lines at even intervals.

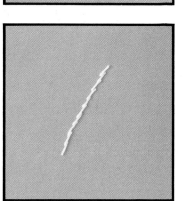

Stem stitch: Pipe short strokes in a line, each stroke overlapping the preceding one slightly.

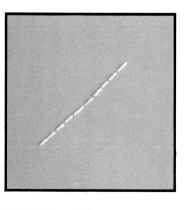

Back stitch: As for running stitch but leave much smaller gaps between 'stitches'.

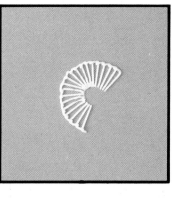

Buttonhole: Pipe a line from left to right then down at a right angle. The second stitch starts inside the corner of the first.

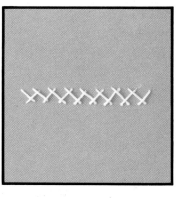

Herringbone: Pipe a diagonal line going down from right to left. Pipe a second diagonal line in the opposite direction which crosses the first towards the bottom of the 'stitch'. The third line crosses the second towards the top.

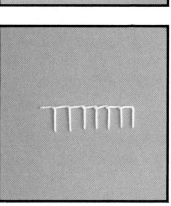

Buttonhole wheel: As for buttonhole but the lines are piped to form a circle. Take care that the right angled lines all point towards the centre.

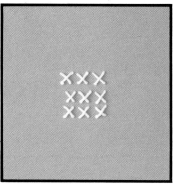

Cross-stitch: Pipe two lines of equal length crossing at the centre.

Fishbone stitch: This is useful for leaves with a central vein. Start at the outside edge of the leaf and pipe an angled line which just crosses the central vein. Pipe the second stitch from the opposite side to cross the vein from the opposite direction.

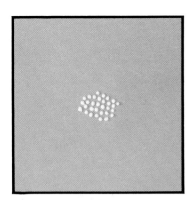

Seed stitch: Pipe very small dots close together. This is useful for flower centres.

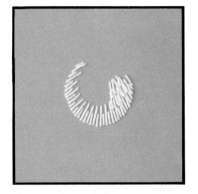

Long and short stitch: Pipe a row of long and short lines. The second row is piped to fill in the gaps.

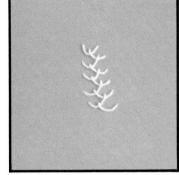

Feather stitch: Pipe a small U-shaped line. Start the second stitch just above the centre of the first and pipe in the opposite direction.

French knots: Pipe a small circle. Continue piping to fill in the centre and pull away in an untidy dot.

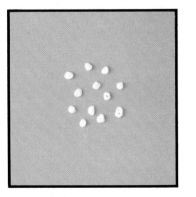

Lazy daisy: Pipe a series of leaf shapes to form a flower. Pipe small lines over the rounded ends.

A selection of freehand piped embroidery designs, suitable for side decorations. Flower patterns can be done in a single colour, as shown, or in different coloured icing. For the initial in the circle, copy letters from the typefaces on page 59, or use letters from embroidery patterns or needle-work books.

Freehand piped designs featuring bows and flowers. Choose patterns which compliment the overall design of the cake. These patterns could also be used individually to decorate small cakes, petits fours or biscuits.

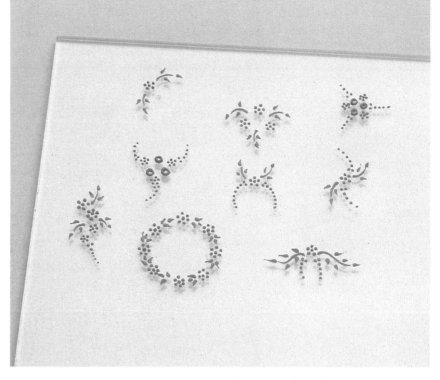

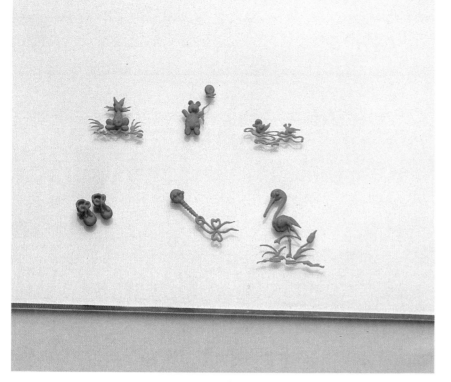

Tiny freehand pressure-piped motifs suitable for side decorations on christening cakes or birthday cakes for young children.

Flower embroidery side designs based on dots and pulled dots.

A selection of the embroidery designs which have been used on the cakes featured in this book.

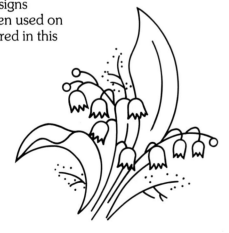

TUBE EMBROIDERY PLAQUE

Trace the design and transfer to a prepared rectangular plaque. Have ready several piping bags with fine tubes filled with the different colour icing. Pipe the design following the embroidery stitches. This kind of design can be adapted to use patterns from books on embroidery and other needlework.

BRODERIE ANGLAISE

This must be done on freshly applied sugarpaste, or sugarpaste which has just skinned, to avoid cracks. The design must be carefully pricked out using a pattern or done freehand. Broderie anglaise can also be done on royal-iced cakes if a sharp scriber is used to make the holes.

Holes are made with the pointed end of a paintbrush, a knitting needle or a special tool. To make oval holes for leaves hold the end of the paintbrush at an angle. Ice around the hole with royal icing.

For coloured embroidery dip the tool into food colouring or petal dust before making the hole. Pipe around the holes using a fine tube and white or coloured icing.

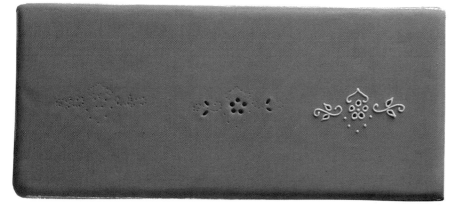

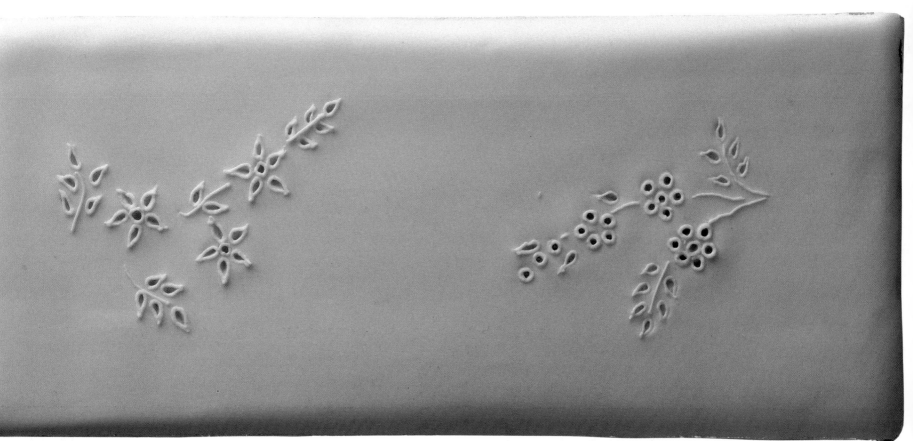

BRODERIE ANGLAISE PLAQUE

Trace the design and transfer to the prepared plaque, which must be soft enough to insert a tool to make the holes. Pipe the design using a fine tube. The icing can be white, as shown, or coloured.

BRUSH EMBROIDERY

This embroidery can be done with soft royal icing but you must work quickly to finish before it dries. Adding about 5ml (1tsp) piping gel to a cup of icing slows down the drying and gives a smoother surface. Use a No1 tube for all embroidery, increasing the pressure where more icing is needed. Always start with the part of the design which appears to be the furthest away, to give depth to the finished work.

Template for the Anemone Cake.

Pipe the outline, working on a small area at a time. Flood just inside the line. Brush the icing down towards the centre of the flower with a small, flat brush which is slightly damp. Continue with each petal, finishing with the one nearest you.

If you use care, it is not necessary to pipe the outlines first. Pipe the line but increase the pressure at the outer edge where you would usually flood it. Always work down towards the point where the petal or leaf is attached to the plant.

When the brush work is completely dry, pipe in any detail, such as stamens in flowers or veins in leaves, using a fine tube. Place the finished plaque in the centre of a plain iced cake.

Template for the brush embroidery plaque shown here.

Template for the brush embroidery Christmas plaque.

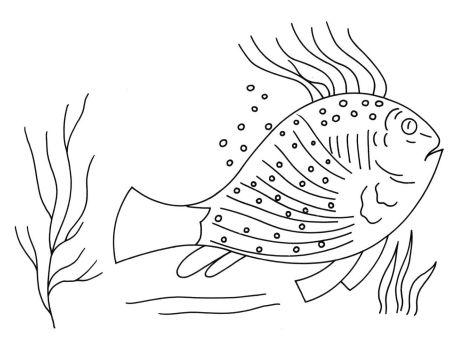

Design for the brush embroidery fish plaque.

TULLE WORK POPPIES

Tulle work involves cutting out shaped pieces of tulle, then piping the design with soft peak royal icing. Leave the pieces to dry over a curved surface if necessary, then attach to a plaque or cake with royal icing. Support until dry.

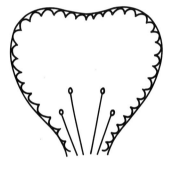

Cut four petals out of red tulle. Pin onto a greased apple tray or press foil into pastry tins and use the foil cups. The petals should be pinned so that the outer edge bends back.

With red royal icing, pipe the design onto the petal and let dry.

Leaves: Cut out leaf shapes. Pipe the design and leave to dry flat or over a slightly curved surface. Pipe the stem directly onto the cake and when leaves are dry arrange them along the stem.

Pipe a blob of green royal icing about 5mm (¼in) in diameter onto the cake. Position the first two petals opposite each other. Support with foam or cotton wool. Place the third and fourth petals inside and on top of the first two. Push the petals into the green blob. Support until dry. Push black stamens into the centre blob as shown.

TULLE WORK KEY

Cut out the key in white tulle and place on a cake board. Cover with wax paper, then pin in position. Pipe the design. When dry, carefully remove from the wax paper, turn over and pipe on the reverse side. Let dry. Attach the key to the top of the 21st birthday cake and support with foam or cotton balls until dry.

TULLE WORK CRADLE

Cut out tulle according to a pattern. Trace around petal cutters to create your design and pin to a cake board over wax paper. Pipe the design and let dry.

Pipe the tulle base quickly onto wax paper and place over a curved surface, such as a kitchen roll tube. Tape each end to the roll.

When dry, attach one end to the base. Lay the outside of the end down on a flat surface. Pipe a line of royal icing in position. Attach base. Make sure it is level or the cradle will tilt. When dry repeat for the other end.

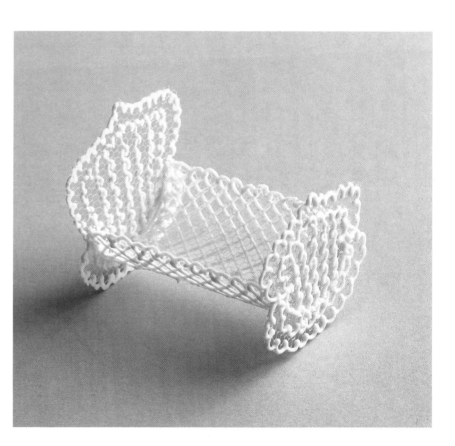

TULLE EXTENSION WORK

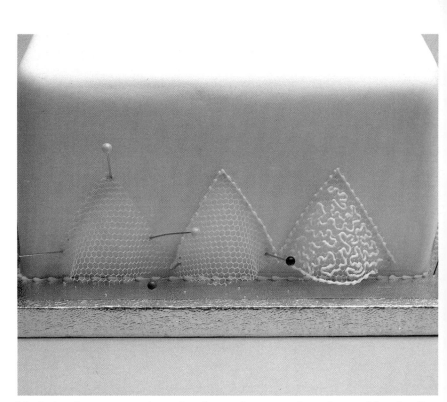

Cut a piece of tulle to the required depth and twice as long as the perimeter or diameter of the cake. Gather so that it fits snugly around the cake. Pin to the surface of the cake, then attach with a snailstrail. Pipe a scallop design at the top and bottom of the tulle, and finish by piping tiny dots on the tulle.

Mark the design onto the side of the cake. Cut tulle triangles slightly larger than the triangle in the design and pin to the cake. Attach with a snailstrail. Remove the pins when dry and finish off each piece with a snailstrail border. Pipe cornelli work on each triangle.

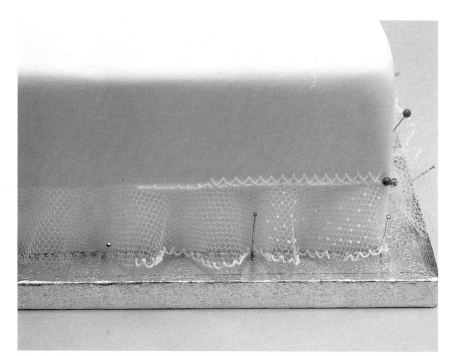

Cut a piece of tulle to the required depth and twice as long as the perimeter or diameter of the cake. Gather so that it fits snugly around the cake. Pin to the surface of the cake, then attach with a snailstrail. Finish off the bottom edge with a snailstrail and the top with scallops. Pipe cornelli work over the tulle.

Pipe the side designs and attach the ribbons first. Cut a piece of tulle to the required depth and twice as long as the perimeter or diameter of the cake. Gather so that it fits snugly around the cake. Pin to the surface, then attach with a snailstrail. Finish off the top with scallops, and pipe two rows of scallops around the bottom. Pipe tiny hearts on the tulle and attach heart lace above it.

FILIGREE PLAQUE CAKE

FLOATING FILIGREE PLAQUE

Trace the wren design and place on a board. Cover with wax paper and tape down. Pipe the background using a No00 tube. First pipe a straight line which goes through the centre of the circle. Turn 90° and pipe a second line at right angles to the first. Turn 90° and pipe a third line which is parallel to the first and 2mm (⅛in) away to the right. Turn 90° and pipe to complete the outline. Continue in this way until the grid is complete. Leave to dry.

Pipe the wren onto the grid lines. When dry, carefully remove from the wax paper and place gently onto a prepared circle of 2cm (¾in) cubes on top of the cake. The cubes should be about 1cm (½in) apart. Pipe lines from the edge of the plaque to the cake, carefully removing the cubes as you go. Pipe drop loops from the edge of the plaque, and position narrow lace around the bottom.

FILIGREE BOX

Do not attempt filigree work on a humid day, as the icing absorbs too much moisture and will not hold its shape. Humidity will also affect the finished article, causing it to bend and, eventually, collapse.

Sections of filigree are piped onto wax paper. If they are to be seen from both sides, when dry turn over and pipe on the reverse side. Using smaller sections with more joins will result in stronger filigree.

Pieces are joined together using royal icing and supported with sugar or stock cubes until dry. Boxes, small blocks of wood, foam or cotton wool can be used for larger items. These supports are used to keep the pieces vertical.

Trace the pattern pieces and put wax paper over them. Pipe the outline of the base. Flood with soft royal icing. Let dry. Pipe two fronts, two sides and four diagonals onto wax paper. Pipe the background with a No00 tube

in an alternating scallop design (like fish scales). Keep the design straight and even. For a quicker design, use a trellis pattern. Pipe the outlines of the birds, flowers and leaves with a No1 tube for contrast, making sure this piping actually touches the background.

Flood the beak, legs, etc and let dry. Carefully release the piped pieces from the wax paper.

Pipe a line of royal icing around the base and join the side pieces. Start at the front and work from side to side, joining pieces at the bottom only. When all the sides are in position, join them together with dots. Support with stock cubes or sugar lumps to ensure sides stay vertical until dry.

Place the top carefully in position and join with dots. If you wish to have the top at an angle, in an open position, support it with cotton wool balls or foam until dry.

Make 2   Make 2

Make 2

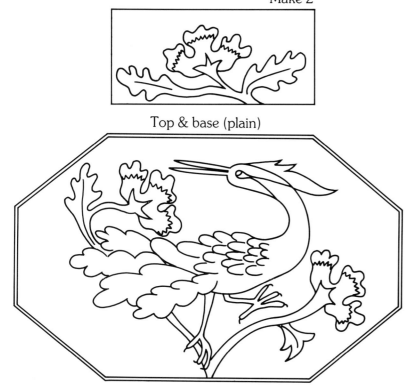

Top & base (plain)

Use a No0 tube to pipe fine designs onto sugared almonds. Straight or diagonal lines, tiny flowers, birds or animals are all suitable. Similar designs could be piped onto sugar cubes, mints or other small sweets.

FILIGREE ANGEL

Pipe the three angel pieces and the lace one or two days in advance, using piping consistency royal icing.

Trace the pattern and place on a flat board. Cover with wax paper taped firmly to the board with masking tape. Pipe the trellis design using a No0 tube and pipe the remaining lines with a No1 tube. Repeat for the other two angels. Let dry. Remove tape to free the wax paper from the board. Carefully pull the paper towards the edges of the board and over the edge using one hand to peel the design away while the other hand holds the paper firm. Turn the paper through 90° and repeat for the other three sides working towards the centre, until the design is free from the paper.

Overpipe on the reverse side, as the angel is seen from all angles. Let dry.

Assembling angel: Take the first angel and pipe a line of icing on the two base points. Position along lines of the circle and support vertically with stock cubes or sugar lumps. Place the other two angels similarly. Join the angels at the centre with criss-crossed lines of icing. Support in position until dry. Pipe a snailstrail or dots along the base to neaten.

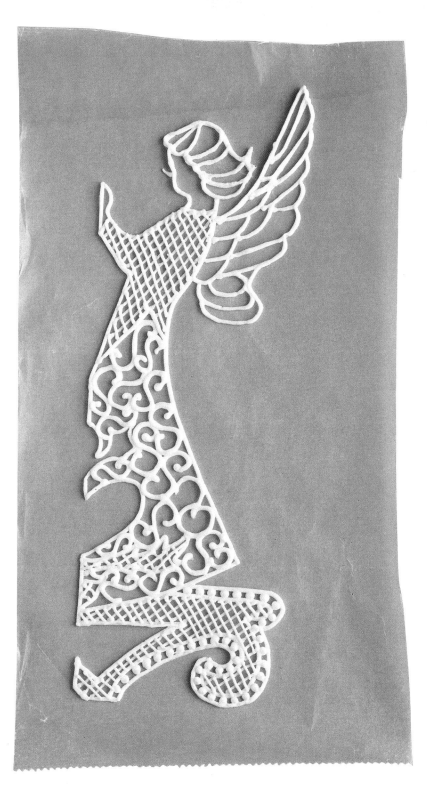

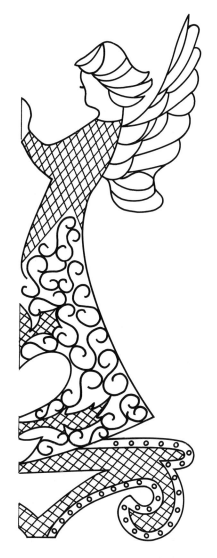

EXTENSION WORK

Use fresh royal icing and No00 or 0 tube for extension work. Always work with the cake at eye level in a good light. Support your back with a small cushion to help prevent backache.

The first step is to pipe the bridgework, a ridge or bridge of icing piped around the edge of the cake from which the drop lines fall. The bridge is a series of drop loops, each row exactly over the preceding one.

To make a pattern for the bridge, measure a band of greaseproof paper the circumference of the cake, fold into sections and cut to the shape of the extension work. This can be scalloped just at the bottom or at the top and bottom. Put this pattern around the cake and mark the lines with a scriber. The bottom edge should be about 5mm (¼in) above the board. Pipe a snailstrail around the base of the cake with a No0.

Work the bridgework with the cake tilted slightly away from you. Touch the tube to the cake at the highest point of the bridge, pull the tube away from the cake and, maintaining even pressure, move the tube horizontally to the next highest point on the design. Touch tube to the cake again.

Work around the cake. Make sure the first row of bridgework is dry before starting on the second. There should be no gaps between the scallops and the cake. If there

are, fill them by painting in soft royal icing with a fine paintbrush. Care must be taken not to pipe each row higher than the one before or an ugly cupped effect will result. Pipe each row exactly over the one preceding, just less than the width of a line.

When the bridge is completely dry, pipe the extension work. Tilt the cake towards you so that the lines fall perpendicularly. Touch the tube to the cake at the top of the design, then pull away immediately, taking care not to get a bulb at the top. Pipe vertical lines just beyond the bridge. Remove the ends with a fine, damp brush. The lines should be parallel and there should not be enough room to pipe another line between the strands.

The simplest form of extension work is done with a straight top and scalloped lower bridge.

Another simple method is from a top line with points, and scallops at the bottom. Try piping dots onto the extension work. This is called hail spotting. Finish off with a triangle of dots, three at the top, then two, then one at the bottom. Pipe a snailstrail at the lower edge.

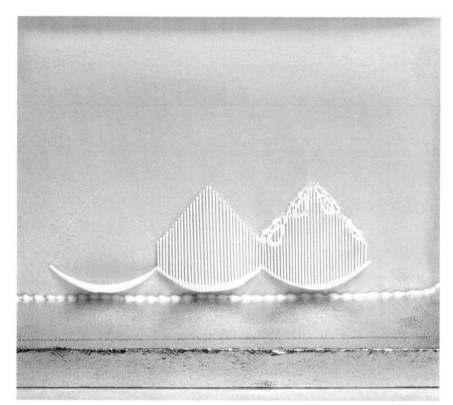

The bridge can be tapered at the sides. Pipe the first line of the bridge over the entire base line, each succeeding line should be piped slightly shorter. Pipe the last line to cover all the other lines. Great care must be taken to make sure each line is shorter by the same amount all around the cake.

For double extension with curtain effect, pipe basic extension work with hail spotting. Then pipe another five lines of bridgework over the first bridge. Tilt the cake towards you and slightly to one side. Pipe a second layer of lines. Finish off the lower edge with drop loops and pulled dots.

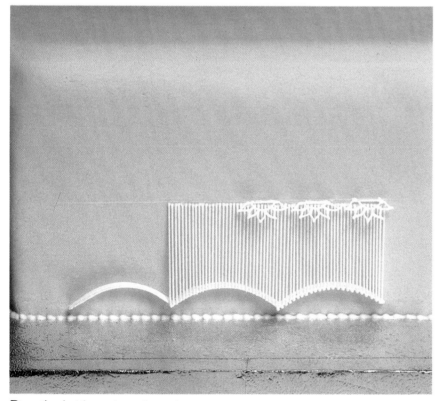

Pipe the bridge when the cake is upsidedown. Attach lace along the top edge and dots along the bottom.

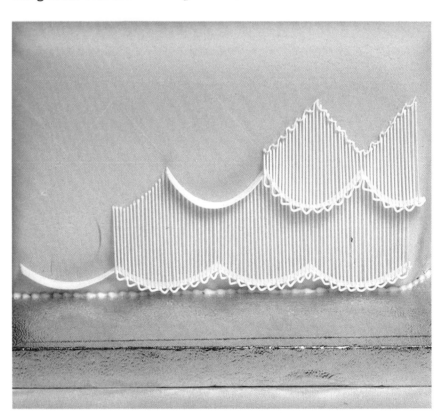

For double extension work, pipe the first bridge and drop lines. Then pipe a second bridge as close as possible to the top of the extension work. Add a second row of extension work. The top and bottom edges are finished with drop loops.

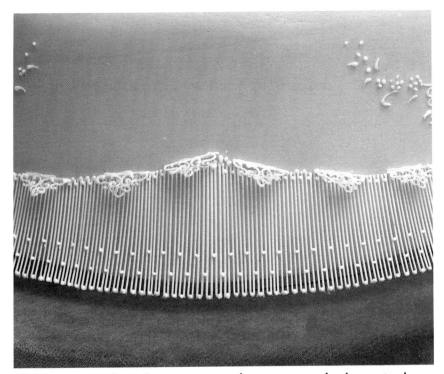

Extension work without a bridge is done by piping from a line on the cake to the rim of a cake tin. When the icing is dry, the cake is removed from on top of the tin and the extension work remains unsupported. For a 20cm (8in) round cake, prepare a 23cm (9in) round cake tin by greasing the rim with white fat and place on the turntable. Put a 15cm (6in) upsidedown tin or dummy in the tin, and position the sugarpasted cake centred on it. The bottom of the cake should be about 5mm (¼in) lower than the rim of the tin. Pipe the extension work, taking great care not to knock the tin. Pipe dots to link each alternate line at the lower edge. Pipe more dots 1cm (½in) up the lines to link and strengthen them. Leave to dry. To remove, place a hand at each side of the cake and lift it straight up. Gently lower onto a prepared board.

TWO-TIER WEDDING CAKE

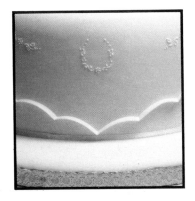

To create the unusual effect of points on the extension work the bridge must be piped with the cake upsidedown. Allow the sugarpaste to dry for at least 48 hours before attempting this or the surface of the cake will be damaged.

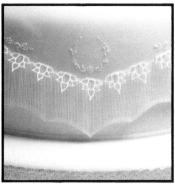

Place a sheet of foam or several layers of smooth, soft cloth on a turntable. Carefully pick up the cake with the fingers of both hands spread out and pointing down. Turn the cake over and lower it onto the pad. Pipe the bridge and let dry. Carefully pick the cake up again, turn it the right way up, and lower it onto a prepared board. The extension work is piped with the cake the right way up using a No00 tube.

PRESSURE PIPING

This is a method for building up three-dimensional piped pictures by increasing or decreasing the amount of pressure. Trace the design and transfer it to a cake or plaque. Look at the original and decide which part should appear to be furthest away, and start piping with that part. Use a bag with a No2 tube, then add details with a smaller tube. Build up the picture, increasing the pressure for parts which need to stand out.

LETTERING TECHNIQUES

Lettering is one of the more problematic aspects of cake decorating, for poor lettering could spoil an otherwise excellent piece of work. Good lettering takes a great deal of practice to achieve.

An experienced decorator will be able to pipe lettering directly onto the cake freehand, but for most people it is best to draw a plan of the cake top and experiment to find the best style, size and position for the letters. The chosen lettering can then be traced and scratched onto the surface of the cake in the correct position before piping.

When piping letters, take care not to form bulbs of icing where lines begin or join. Neaten any ugly joins with a dampened paintbrush. If letters are still imperfect, overpipe the lines with very small dots or a fine snailstrail using a No0 or 00 tube.

When piping on a sugarpasted cake, be careful not to rest your hand on the edge of the cake, as this may spoil the surface. Instead, rest your forearm on a turntable slightly higher than the cake and positioned just to the side.

Piping directly onto the cake with a strong colour can be risky, as the colour will stain the surface, making it difficult to correct mistakes. A better method is to pipe the lettering first in icing to match the basecoat, and then overpipe with the chosen colour icing.

Lettering can also be done with runouts on wax paper and then positioned on the cake with royal icing when dry. This is more suitable for doing numbers or initials than for greetings.

PLAQUES WITH INSCRIPTIONS

The plaques here are inscribed with the greetings shown on page 60. Prepare sugarpaste plaques, then transfer the chosen lettering. Pipe the lettering. Finish off the plaque with piped flowers or other designs, or pressure pipe figures. If wished, the plaque can be removed before the cake is cut and either saved as a momento or stored and used again.

ABCDEFGH
IJKLMNOPQ
RSTUVW
XYZ

c bcdefghijkl
noparstuv
wxyz

12345
67890

ABCDEFG
HIJKLM
NOPQRS
TUVWXYZ

abcdefghij
klmnopqr
stuvwxyz

12345
67890

Happy
Birthday

Welcome
Baby

Merry
Christmas

New Year
Greetings

Happy
Anniversary

Good
Luck

Happy
Birthday

Easter
Greetings

Congratulations

1234567890

1234567890

1234567890

A B C D E
F G H I J K
L M N O P
Q R S T U
V W X Y Z

a b c d e f g h i j
k l m n o p q r
s t u v w x y z

a d e h i k
m n t u w

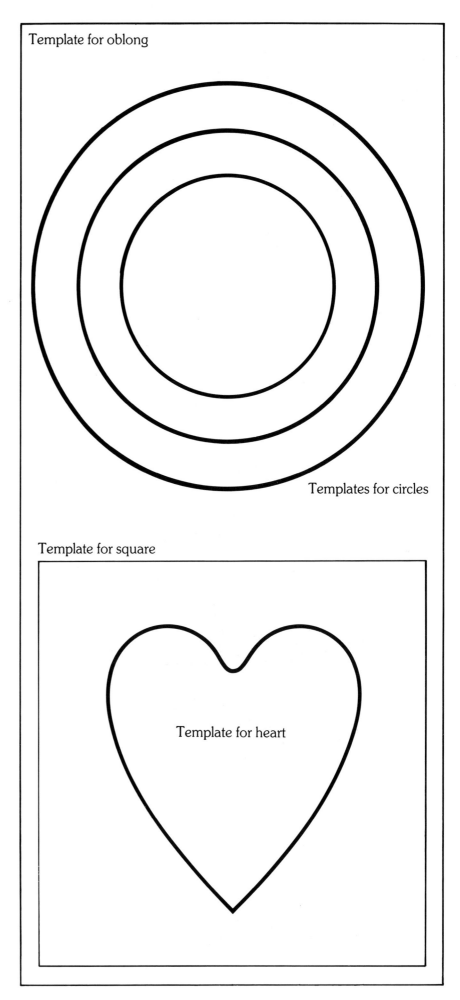

Template for oblong

Templates for circles

Template for square

Template for heart

INSTRUCTIONS
FOR CAKES

Cornelli work cake: Cover the cake with coffee-coloured sugarpaste. Scribe the design onto the cake. With a No0 tube pipe cornelli work with cream-coloured royal icing. Pipe snailstrail around all edges except the flower. Outline the flower with a No1 tube. The centre of the flower is worked with pulled dots and then filled in with dark brown dots. Pipe a dark brown snailstrail all around the outer edge of the design. Work the design on the side of the cake similarly over the ribbon. Pipe a bottom border of cornelli work topped with a dark brown snailstrail. Pipe shells around the bottom edge of the cake. Overpipe each shell with brown S-shapes. Pipe a scratch line on the cake board around each shell.

Basket weave cake: Basket work can be done either with plain or basket weave tubes. When covering a square or on the sides of the cake, pipe a vertical line with a plain tube. Pipe horizontally over the top of this line with a basket weave tube. Start 1.5cm (½in) in front of the vertical line and extend to 2cm (¾in) beyond it. Leave a gap the width of the basket weave line, and then pipe another line. Continue in this way until you reach the bottom. Now pipe a second vertical line with the writing tube, parallel to the first and 1.5cm (½in) away. With a basket weave tube, repeat as for previous line but pipe in the gaps. When dry position a ribbon and decorate with piped buttercream roses.

Autumn leaves birthday cake: Make the borders and collars following the instructions on page 40. Coat a 20cm (8in) oval cake with gold-coloured royal icing. Coat an oblong board with the same icing. Attach the ribbons. Position the collars and borders. Neaten the bottom edge with a snailstrail and pipe the inscription.

Greenhouse cake: Cover the cake with green sugarpaste. Mark the plan of the greenhouse on the cake. Make the path with grey sugarpaste and mark the tiles. Use brown royal icing for the earth and rough the surface with a palette knife. Position the toothpick tomato plants and lower the greenhouse into place over them. Use grey sugarpaste for the crazy paving, marking the stones in a random pattern. Make the vegetable garden and flower patch and position the fruit and vegetables. Lettuces are made as green 'roses' and carrots are blobs of orange icing with green pulled dots at the top. Tomatoes are red dots.

Twenty-first birthday cake: Cover the cake in pale green sugarpaste. Place an oval of pink sugarpaste on top, outline with a pattern of three dots piped in a triangle; two at the bottom and one on top. Pipe lace: long, medium and short. Pipe embroidery onto the cake. Attach ribbon at the bottom and at a distance up the cake equal to the depth of the long lace. Attach the lace, supporting it with foam or cotton balls if necessary. Attach the key to the top with royal icing. Support until dry. An easier way to do the key is to pipe it flat, directly onto the cake.

Sleeping mouse cake: This cake would be suitable for either a birthday or a christening. Coat a 20cm (8in) round cake with pale green royal icing, and coat the board with the same icing. Make the top and base collars following the instructions on page 23. The template for the top design is on page 26. Pipe the designs on the side. Position the base collars and neaten the edges with a snailstrail. Attach the top collars with royal icing and pipe dots on the inner edge. Place flowers between each collar.

Anemone cake: Cover a round cake with cream sugarpaste. Do the template on page 44. Pipe the tassel border in cream and overpipe in colours to match the embroidery.

Filigree plaque cake: Cover a round cake with pale lilac sugarpaste. Place on an iced cake card and position on a velvet-covered board. Pipe the side designs. Do the extension work without a bridge. Pipe the floating filigree wren plaque and position. Add lace.

Two-tier wedding cake: Cover the two oval cakes in cream sugarpaste. Position ribbons and side designs. The pointed extension work has a yellow bridge and white drop lines. Finish off with lace. Make the sugar flower sprays in complimentary colours.

Angel Christmas cake: Make approximately 40 pieces of snowflake lace (32 pieces will actually be used.) Cover the cake with blue sugarpaste. Pipe shells around the base with a No6 tube.

Mark a circle in the centre of the cake and draw lines to divide into thirds. Pipe snowflakes randomly over the cake either freehand or by first scribing the design onto the cake. Make the angels and position in the centre.

Attach lace in a random pattern to the sides and in the circle around angels on the top of the cake.